A Year at Monticello
—1795—

Front view of Monticello, commissioned by Ellen Randolph Coolidge and painted by Jane Bradick in 1825. Courtesy of the Thomas Jefferson Memorial Foundation, Inc.

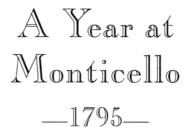

A Year at Monticello
—1795—

Donald Jackson

FULCRUM, INC.
GOLDEN, COLORADO

Library of Congress Cataloging-in-Publication Data

Jackson, Donald Dean, 1919–1987
    A year at Monticello, 1795.

      Bibliography: p.
      1. Jefferson, Thomas, 1743–1826—Homes and haunts—
Virginia—Albemarle County. 2. Monticello (Va.)
3. Plantation life—Virginia—Albemarle County—History
—18th century. 4. Albemarle County (Va.)—Social
life and customs.   I. Title.
E332.74.J33   1989   975.5'482   89-7847
ISBN 1-55591-050-5

Printed in the United States of America
9 8 7 6 5 4 3 2 1

Fulcrum, Inc.
Golden, Colorado

Table of Contents

Publisher's Preface

D onald Jackson had completed the manuscript for *A Year at Monticello: 1795* before his death in 1987. Except for minor editorial changes, the text is published here as he wrote it. In addition, citations have been included indicating sources of the quotations, using Jackson's own notes whenever possible, and his "Note on Sources" has been updated with recent publications.

We are grateful to his widow, Cathie Jackson, for permission to publish this material, and for her assistance in supplying Donald Jackson's notes. We are also grateful to his friend, James P. Ronda, professor of history at Youngstown State University, for his introduction. We appreciate the research and editorial support provided by Maxine Benson, who holds a doctorate in history from the University of Colorado.

We also acknowledge the Thomas Jefferson Memorial Foundation, the Alderman Library of the University of Virginia, the Massachusetts Historical Society and the White House Historical Association for their assistance in providing appropriate illustrations to accompany the text.

Donald Jackson: An Appreciation

James P. Ronda

onald Jackson once wrote that he imagined his task to be that of a polisher of others' words and thoughts. As longtime editor at the University of Illinois Press, he guided scores of scholarly books along the trail from idea to print. And as one of the finest documentary editors in this century, he rescued and restored the words of Meriwether Lewis, William Clark, Zebulon Montgomery Pike, John C. Frémont, and George Washington. But as was so often the case, Don was far too modest about his own contributions. He did far more than advance the wisdom of others. By his life and in his work he en-

3

livened the entire enterprise of American exploration history. Along the way he set a high standard for documentary editing.

Little in Don's boyhood seemed to mark him out as one of this country's foremost western historians. Born into a hard-working Iowa farm family, Don spent his early years following the plow and dreaming of a larger world. While other Mills County boys plotted ways to reach Omaha or Chicago, Don made regular pilgrimages to the local Carnegie Library. He once described that venerable institution as his Library of Congress. The modest brick building just off the Glenwood town square nourished the life of the mind and showed Don a world far beyond farm fields and seed catalogs.

During the late 1930s Don waged a fierce struggle to get a college education. A slender Sears, Roebuck scholarship sent him to Iowa State University. At Ames he used every bit of ingenuity to stretch those hard-won dollars. It was at Iowa State that Don learned the craft of journalism. His humor columns for the college newspaper made him a campus personality, as did his novel, *Archer Pilgrim*. The journalist's eye and the novelist's deft touch for dialogue would stay with him throughout his career. They would enrich all he wrote.

What might have been a modest career in radio broadcasting and agricultural journalism was abruptly halted by the events of December 7, 1941. Don's brother Robert was on board the USS *Arizona,* and his death brought the war home with tragic force. After finishing his degree at Iowa State, Don enlisted in the Navy and soon became an officer in a naval intelligence and communications unit. Those wartime experiences became the subject for his last full-length book, *Torokina: A Wartime Memoir, 1941–1945.*

At war's end Don and his wife Cathie returned to Iowa, this time to the University of Iowa. There Don pursued a graduate program of his own design—one that combined journalism, fine printing, and scholarly publishing. It was a course of study that suited a man whose interests ranged from exotic woods to ancient coins. From 1948 to 1968 Don was editor at the University of Illinois Press at Urbana-Champaign. There he not only shepherded academic monographs but also began a long series of distinguished documentary projects. His *Letters of the Lewis and Clark Expedition, The Journals of Zebulon Montgomery Pike,* and (with Mary Lee Spence) *The Expeditions of John Charles Frémont* not only revitalized the study of western exploration but marked Don as an editor of extraordinary skill and sensitivity.

In 1968 the Jacksons left Urbana-Champaign for Charlottesville, Virginia, where Don became founding editor of the new University of Virginia Papers of George Washington project. By the time he retired in 1977, Don had seen to publication the first six volumes of the Washington papers. In addition, he had laid the groundwork for his important *Thomas Jefferson and the Stony Mountains*. A lifetime of research and writing did not stop with retirement. From his mountain home outside Colorado Springs, Don wrote four more books. He not only pursued his own work, but through a vast correspondence taught and encouraged younger scholars.

When Don Jackson died in December 1987 he left behind an unpublished manuscript. He had been thinking for some time about a book comparing the farming pursuits of Washington and Jefferson. What better way to understand their world than to look at the land that was the foundation of it all? *A Year at Monticello—1795* was the beginning of what surely would have been a memorable book. Don believed that history came alive in its small details. He always counseled writers to find those telling incidents, those bits of the past that might illuminate the larger whole. Don had a journalist's eye for such detail. Whether it was a prairie plant or the shape of a distant mountain peak, Don caught it all and made it live again. Nowhere is that passion for getting just the right color and shape of experience more plain than in his last essay. Here we see Jefferson watching after every aspect of a complex plantation community. Animals, seeds, weather, and the texture of the land are all laid open for us to rediscover. As Jefferson filled his farm and garden books with every change on his land, so Don took those fragments of evidence and made a lost world live again.

Writing about Jefferson and Monticello's good earth, Don came full circle to his own Iowa roots. As a lonely student at Iowa State he had once stood quietly in the cattle barns just to breathe the smells of home. Don knew firsthand the daily rhythm of planting, nurturing, and harvesting. He wrote this essay with the double authority of personal experience and thorough archival research. Here Don brought back to life a forgotten Monticello, not only a place of great ideas but also a home with friends and gardens. In his essay Jefferson's mountain house moves from textbook history to living memory. By invoking the rituals of sun and rain, earth and sky, Don gives us a Monticello that finds a place in the heart as well as the mind. Such was the final gift from an Iowa farm boy with the West in his eyes.

Donald Jackson's Publications

I ncluded in the following listing are the books and articles written or edited by Donald Jackson during his long and distinguished career. The bibliography does not include material from his years as a university student, when he was producing articles, stories, and columns both for sale and for use in student publications.

BOOKS, INCLUDING DOCUMENTARY EDITIONS
Torokina: A Wartime Memoir, 1941-1945. Ames: Iowa State University Press, 1989.
Among the Sleeping Giants: Occasional Pieces on Lewis and Clark. Urbana: University of Illinois Press, 1987.

Voyages of the Steamboat Yellow Stone. New York: Ticknor and Fields, 1985. Paperback edition, Norman: University of Oklahoma Press, 1987.

Valley Men: A Speculative Account of the Arkansas Expedition of 1807. New York: Ticknor and Fields, 1983.

Thomas Jefferson and the Stony Mountains: Exploring the West from Monticello. Urbana: University of Illinois Press, 1981.

The Diaries of George Washington (with Dorothy Twohig). 6 vols. Charlottesville: University Press of Virginia, 1976-79.

George Washington and the War of Independence. Williamsburg: Virginia Independence Bicentennial Commission, 1976.

The Expeditions of John Charles Frémont (with Mary Lee Spence). 2 vols. in 4 parts. Urbana: University of Illinois Press, 1970-73. (Vol. 3 continued by Spence alone, 1984.)

The Journals of Zebulon Montgomery Pike, with Letters and Related Documents. 2 vols. Norman: University of Oklahoma Press, 1966.

Custer's Gold: The United States Cavalry Expedition of 1874. New Haven: Yale University Press, 1966.

Letters of the Lewis and Clark Expedition, 1783-1854, with Related Documents. Urbana: University of Illinois Press, 1962. Revised edition, 1978.

Johann Amerbach. Iowa City: The Prairie Press, 1959.

Black Hawk: An Autobiography. Urbana: University of Illinois Press, 1955. Also various paperback editions.

Archer Pilgrim (a novel). New York: Dodd, Mead and Co., 1942.

ARTICLES

"The West." In *Thomas Jefferson: A Reference Biography*, edited by Merrill D. Peterson. New York: Charles Scribner's Sons, 1986.

Foreword to *Travels in the Interior of America in the Years 1809, 1810, and 1811*, by John Bradbury. Lincoln: University of Nebraska Press, 1986.

"Call Him a Good Old Dog, But Don't Call Him Scannon." *We Proceeded On* (July 1985):2-8. Reprinted as Publication 2A, Lewis and Clark Trail Heritage Foundation, Inc.

"What I Did for Love—of Editing." *Western Historical Quarterly* 13 (July 1982):291-97.

"Jefferson, Meriwether Lewis, and the Reduction of the United States Army." *Proceedings of the American Philosophical Society* 124 (April 1980):91-96.

"Zebulon Pike's Damned Rascals." *Occasional Papers, No. 1*, Pikes Peak Posse of the Westerners, Colorado Springs (1979):1-8.

Introduction to *Narrative of a Journey Across the Rocky Mountains to the Columbia River, 1839*, by John Kirk Townsend. Lincoln: University of Nebraska Press, 1978.

"Ledyard and Lapérouse: A Contrast in Northwestern Exploration." *Western Historical Quarterly* 9 (October 1978):495-508.

"Zebulon Pike—the Poor Man's Lewis and Clark." *We Proceeded On* (October 1978):6-9.

The Papers of George Washington in the Bicentennial Year (published lectures). Staunton, Va.: Mary Baldwin College, 1977.

"George Washington's Beautiful Nelly." *American Heritage* 28 (February 1977):80-85.

"The Editor's Other Functions." In *The Publication of American Historical Manuscripts,* edited by Leslie W. Dunlap and Fred Shelley. Iowa City: University of Iowa Libraries, 1976.

"Thomas Jefferson and the Pacific Northwest." *We Proceeded On* (Winter, 1974-75):5-8.

"A Footnote to the Lewis and Clark Expedition." *Manuscripts* 24 (Winter 1972):3-21.

Foreword to *George Washington: A Biography,* edited by Ralph K. Andrist. New York: Newsweek Books, 1972.

"Starting in the Papers Game." *Scholarly Publishing* 3 (October 1971):28-38.

Foreword to *In the Footsteps of Lewis and Clark,* edited by Gerald S. Snyder. Washington, D.C.: National Geographic Society, 1970.

"The Papers of George Washington: A Year of Beginnings." *Reports,* Washington Association of New Jersey, Morristown, February 23, 1970.

"The Papers of George Washington." *Manuscripts* 22 (Winter 1970):3-11.

"On Reading Lewis and Clark: A Bibliographical Essay." *Montana, the Magazine of Western History* 18 (Summer 1968):2-7.

"Some Advice for the Next Editor of Lewis and Clark." *Bulletin of the Missouri Historical Society* 24 (October 1967):52-62.

"The Myth of the Frémont Howitzer." *Bulletin of the Missouri Historical Society* 23 (April 1967):205-14.

"The American *Entrada*: A Spanish Point of View." In *The Frontier Re-Examined*, edited by John Francis McDermott. Urbana: University of Illinois Press, 1967.

"Zebulon M. Pike 'Tours' Mexico." *American West* 3 (Summer 1966):67-71, 89-93.

"The Public Image of Lewis and Clark." *Pacific Northwest Quarterly* 57 (January 1966):1-7.

"How Lost Was Zebulon Pike?" *American Heritage* 16 (February 1965):10-15. Reprinted in *The American Heritage Book of Great Adventures of the Old West.* New York: American Heritage Press, 1969.

"On the Death of Meriwether Lewis's Servant." *William and Mary Quarterly* 21 (July 1964):445-48.

"Journey to the Mandans, 1809: The Lost Narrative of Dr. Thomas." *Bulletin of the Missouri Historical Society* 20 (April 1964):179-92.

"My Secretary, Meriwether Lewis." *Westerners Brand Book,* New York Posse 10 (No. 2 1963):38-41.

"Black Hawk—The Man and His Times" and "Black Hawk—The Last Campaign." *Palimpsest* 43 (February 1962):65-94.

"The Race to Publish Lewis and Clark." *Pennsylvania Magazine of History and Biography* 85 (April 1961): 163-77.

"Boards and Buckram." A quarterly column, 1961-63, in *Scholarly Books in America,* a publication of the Association of American University Presses.

"Lewis and Clark among the Oto." *Nebraska History* 41 (September 1960):237-48.

"Old Fort Madison, 1808-1813." *Palimpsest* 39 (January 1958):1-64. Republished with additions, 47 (January 1966):1-62.

"William Ewing, Agricultural Agent to the Indians." *Agricultural History* 31 (April 1957):3-7.

"Too Much to Lose" (a short story). *Redbook,* November 1952.

A Year at
Monticello: 1795

The East Front of Monticello. Courtesy of the Thomas Jefferson Memorial Foundation, Inc. (photograph by James Tkatch).

Introduction

In the Piedmont region of Virginia, lying between Tidewater on the east and the Blue Ridge Mountains on the west, a little farming goes on throughout the winter. Snows come and quickly melt, and plowshares gouge the brick-red soil even in January and February while farmers farther north are weeks away from treading the freshly turned earth.

In 1795, however, the winter in the neighborhood of Monticello was wretched. Thomas Jefferson, whose plowmen had for one reason or another skimped on their work the previous fall, despaired of getting the fields ready for the spring planting. From the "little hill" where his Palladian mansion had long been abuilding, he could stand in January at the east entrance of the house and see several of his fields, including those lying beyond the Rivanna River below, and watch the soil drying rapidly into plowing condition. Then next day would come rain or snow and another delay.

It was Jefferson's second year at home during a hiatus from government that he swore was to last forever. The year was to be so uneventful, so un-Jeffersonian, that an early family biographer later brushed it aside as meriting no attention. His great-granddaughter, Sarah N. Randolph, writing *The Domestic Life of Thomas Jefferson,* declared that she found "nothing worthy of notice in Jefferson's life during the year 1795."[1]

Many of the Founding Fathers were caught between a nagging realization that they must serve the nation they had wrought, and a longing for a calmer life at home—a home that very often was a plantation or farm. George Washington himself set the pattern by declining, accepting, changing his mind, and grousing throughout his professional life that he would rather be riding acros· his fields than leading an army or fine-tuning a new kind of government. It was almost routine for a man entering or reentering public life to assert dolefully that he did so with grave doubts and after long deliberation. Jefferson more than once expressed his own preference by saying he would rather be sick in bed at Monticello than hale and chipper anywhere else.

For whatever reasons—family problems, a yearning for the rural life, or a reluctance to be bloodied in the political fray—Jefferson was slow to adjust to the routines of public service. After several years in the Virginia Assembly, an assignment close to home and not very arduous, he was named in 1775 to his first national position, a seat from Virginia in the Continental Congress. He spent the first four months of 1776 at home, a difficult period to reconstruct; he stopped writing letters, even stopped making entries in his beloved garden book where he usually recorded the plantings and harvestings. He resigned from Congress that year, spending six years absent from the national scene. He returned to it only after his wife, Martha, died in 1782, having borne six children, of whom only two—the girls he now cherished—survived.

He continued on, however, in commonwealth affairs. Jefferson's election as wartime governor of Virginia in 1779 came at a difficult time, and he was both unhappy and ineffective in that office. He resigned in 1781, telling Edmund Randolph, "I have taken my final leave of every thing of that nature, have retired to my farm, my family and books from which I think nothing will ever more separate me."[2] He also resigned from the Virginia House of Delegates and declined to serve further in the Continental Congress.

According to Randolph, Jefferson seemed to have an "unpardonable rage for retirement."[3] But many of his colleagues in and out of government might well have believed that an ambivalent Jefferson was far better than a dogged political hack who never missed a roll call. During these early, erratic years from 1775 to 1784 he produced his first published work, *A Summary View of the Rights of British America;* drafted the Declaration of Independence, the Virginia Constitution, and a Virginia bill for establishing religious freedom; and laid the groundwork for the orderly opening of the West by his role in formulating the Northwest Ordinance.

Reluctantly, as usual, he allowed himself to be named minister plenipotentiary to France in 1784, to negotiate trade agreements. By now the care of his two daughters, teen-aged Martha and six-year-old Maria, was much on his mind. He took Martha with him to Europe, sailing that summer with two slaves

Thomas Jefferson's Library. The volumes on display here are duplicates of those once owned by Jefferson. His original collection was sold to the federal government in 1815 and became the nucleus of the present Library of Congress. The architect's table was made in the Monticello cabinet shop. Courtesy of the Thomas Jefferson Memorial Foundation, Inc. (photograph by James Tkatch).

and leaving Maria in the care of her aunt, Elizabeth Eppes. The little girl was sent to join him later, and both daughters were placed in school at the Abbaye Royale de Panthémont. Jefferson soon succeeded Benjamin Franklin as regular minister to France, and spent more than five years there, developing an abiding penchant for all things French, traveling briefly to Italy, and watching his girls become charming young women.

It may have been Martha's growing fascination with the quiet allurements of life in a Catholic convent that caused Jefferson to ask for a leave of absence in 1789, to bring his daughters home. Arriving in Norfolk with the expectation of returning soon to Europe, he was advised that President George Washington had named him to become the first secretary of state. Jefferson wrote one of his "I'd rather not" letters to Washington, explaining that he was satisfied in France and pointing out his unfitness for the secretaryship. "I should enter on it with gloomy forebodings," he said, but would abide by "whatever you may be pleased to decide."[4] He thus backed into another important government position that he thought he did not want.

Martha soon married Thomas Mann Randolph, a future governor of Virginia, and became the mistress of Monticello while her husband rode the fields and provided Jefferson with firsthand reports on agricultural matters. Maria (christened Mary but called Maria and sometimes Polly) once again lived with her aunt and seemed to be an adored but neglected pawn of the various moves of her father.

Possibly Jefferson accepted his new assignment with the resolve to stay only long enough to quiet the pressure from the president and get the secretaryship organized. Less than two months after he had assumed office, his son-in-law Thomas was writing about the "prospect of your retiring, which we anxiously expect."[5]

After serving two years, during which he spent seven months at home, Jefferson was chafing to escape. He told Washington in May 1792 that he did not want to serve another term, although he hoped that Washington himself would continue as president. He wrote his close friend James Madison that the motion of his blood no longer kept time with the tumult of the world, and that "it leads me to seek for happiness in the lap and love of my family."[6]

Only the need to support the president during a difficult time, when the United States was trying to remain neutral during a war between England and France, kept Jefferson in office through 1793. His final year was spent gearing up for the life of a progressive farmer. He talked crop rotation and livestock breeding, and sketched out new arrangements for his fields. When it appeared that he must stay in office through the whole year, he wrote in frustration to Martha that "I have for some time past been under an agitation of mind which I scarcely ever experienced before."[7] He was sorely tried by the behavior of Edmond Charles Genêt, the new young minister to the United States. As the first diplomatic representative of the French Republic, Genêt appeared after England and France had declared war and the United States was trying hard to remain neutral. He was determined to commit Washington to support France, and among his upstart notions was a plan to enlist western citizens in hostile acts against Spain. As if to make 1793 entirely memorable in a depressing way, the gods laid upon Philadelphia that summer an outbreak of yellow fever that sent government members to Germantown to await cooler weather and a slackening of the truly devastating, frightening disease.

As a hardworking member and future president of the American Philosophical Society, Jefferson led a subscription to send botanist André Michaux to the Pacific Ocean. Disappointment came when Michaux turned out to be a part of the Genêt intrigue and either was recalled or decided to return voluntarily to the East.

Jefferson's hunger to resume farming was genuine enough, and he seemed convinced, as he wrote Colonel David Humphreys, that he was worn down with drudgery, "while every circumstance relative to my private affairs calls imperiously for my return to them."[8] There was more to his impatience, however, and it revealed an aspect of his nature that some of his colleagues and most of his biographers saw clearly. He was, as someone has said, the kind of man who would have loved to play chess by correspondence, but he tended to shy away from verbal, head-on confrontations. Not the kind of person to rise up red-faced in public and declaim, "Give me liberty or give me death." And so when his old opponent and critic Alexander Hamilton, the secretary of the treasury, began to score too many points and—as Jefferson believed—to win the heart and mind of Washington to the Federalist cause, it was time to back off once more. The suspicion among supporters of republicanism that Hamilton was campaigning to run Jefferson out of office made his friends even more determined that he stay. To thwart this friendly plotting, he burned his bridges by giving up his living quarters and shipping all his books home.

He left Philadelphia (which had replaced New York as the national capital) at the beginning of 1794. To prove to himself and others that he was home to stay, he had made a single trip to Richmond that spring, then dug in at Monticello. He boasted that he received no Philadelphia newspapers and did not need them, relying on correspondents to keep him informed on political matters. He was happy to be in the fields or planning the long-awaited reconstruction of the mansion. He resumed the keeping of weather observations, a lifelong habit, and recorded that the temperature was below freezing about half the mornings in January 1794. Before the year was out he would decline a special mission to Spain and watch from afar as Hamilton persuaded Washington to put down the Whiskey Rebellion in western Pennsylvania. His eye was on the furrow and he would not meddle. To Washington he wrote only of agricultural matters:

> I find on a more minute examination of my lands than the short visits heretofore made to them permitted, that a ten years' abandonment of them to the ravages of overseers, has brought on them a degree of degradation far beyond what I had expected.[9]

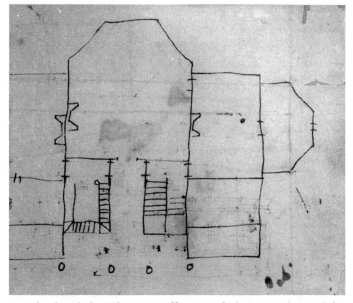

Rough sketch by Thomas Jefferson of changes planned for
Monticello. Courtesy of the University of Virginia, Alderman
Library.

In short, he told another correspondent, he had found his farms "in a state of barbarism."

To Congressman James Madison, whose home was less than a day's ride into Orange County, he sent in the spring of 1794 the only kind of news he hoped to convey for a long time. He said he had heard the year's first whippoorwill during the night.

January and February

M artha and her husband had moved downriver
to their plantation, Varina, below Richmond,
and Jefferson was again master of Monticello. If there
was a woman of the house now, it was tall and
comely Maria, who at sixteen was helping to care for
Martha's two small children that Jefferson was keeping for the year. The elder was little Anne Cary Randolph, with a birthday coming soon that would make
her four, and the other Thomas Jefferson Randolph,
who would be three in the fall.

Slaves were everywhere, more than a hundred,
populating the house and grounds, some living in

cabins on Mulberry Row not far from the mansion, others dispersed on the farms at Shadwell and Lego across the Rivanna. Most had well-defined roles, and among themselves maintained a kind of class system based in part on their duties and partly on their seniority, proven loyalty, or sheer appeal to the Jefferson family. There were body servants, house servants, cooks, artisans, and, at the bottom of the scale, the field hands. There also was a special inner family of slaves, a matriarchy headed by mulatto Betty Hemings, which would eventually include twelve children. Betty had come to Monticello as part of Martha Jefferson's dowry, and apparently six of her offspring were sired by her former owner John Wayles, the father of Jefferson's late wife. Of her better known children, Sally, who in her teens had been with Jefferson and his children in France, was now a house servant and seamstress. Another Hemings was James, who had been with Jefferson in France, learned the art of French cookery, and was to be freed as soon as he had taught his younger brother Peter what he had learned. John Hemings was a skilled artisan and cabinetmaker. Another son, Robert, had recently been freed. Most of these Hemings children were "bright" mulattoes, fair enough to pass as Caucasians.

Isaac Jefferson, one of the many slaves born at Monticello. Courtesy of the University of Virginia, Alderman Library (daguerreotype by John Plumbe, circa 1845).

Other slaves important to the functioning of
Monticello at this time included Jupiter, Jefferson's
old body servant since college days; Davy, who used
to travel alone to Philadelphia carrying goods and
messages; Tom Shackleford, another trusted messen-
ger; Great George, so called to distinguish him from
other Georges in the slave family; and his wife Ursula, who had come with the dowry and was the servant usually entrusted with the keys to the wine and
cider cellars. All these residents of the mansion and
the cabins supported each other through the unplea-
santness of winter, kept a couple of dozen fireplaces
blazing, nursed their colds, and waited for good
plowing weather to bring a focus into their lives.

So lived this man to whom slavery was a mill-
stone, a hair shirt, and a "fatal stain" on the Old South,
which he had concluded must be the heritage of at
least one more generation. Jefferson was generally a
benevolent slavemaster, known to have permitted
certain slaves to "escape" by simply walking off the
premises without pursuit. He seldom sold slaves, but
James Monroe at nearby Ash Lawn had not fully paid
him for Thenia Hemings and her children, who had
been sold to him last year. It is not clear why Jefferson
made an exception here, but it has been suggested
that the father of Thenia's children was already

owned by Monroe. She was Sally Hemings's sister, twenty-seven years old.

Hugh Petit, one of the white overseers, was supervising the grubbing of eight acres of new farmland and cutting fence rails. At the end of the month, Jacob Silkknitter was coming to start burning a year's supply of charcoal for the forges. It was a holding time: keep warm, try to stay well, and wait.

Jefferson's fascination with his little grandson was a new experience for him. The child was hearty and loud, "robust as a beef," refusing to wear shoes until his grandfather designed a pair of moccasins that could be laced on firmly. "He has not worn his shoes an hour this winter. If put on him, he takes them off immediately and uses one to carry his nuts etc. in."[10] So ran one report to Martha, down at Varina. When his parents sent him a wooden gun, he broke it within three hours and used the barrel as a stick with which to poke the fire. The colds that he and Anne were having set their grandfather to thinking of installing cast-iron stoves in the living quarters to supplement the fireplaces.

If little Jeffy showed a flaw of character at this time, a flaw at least in his grandfather's eyes, it was his fear of dogs. The solution was age-old; in January a puppy was brought in to romp with the boy, in a

The parlor at Monticello was probably one of the rooms in which Jefferson considered installing cast-iron stoves. The parquet floor, designed by Jefferson, is believed to be the first of its kind in the United States. The squares are of cherry bordered by beechwood. Courtesy of the Thomas Jefferson Memorial Foundation, Inc. (photograph by James Tkatch).

household where dogs were never kept inside, and there was hope that the scheme would work.

The grandchildren were going to thrive; it was daughter Maria about whom Jefferson might have worried. He demanded unswerving love from his daughters, while holding them to impossibly exacting standards of demeanor and awesome rigors of learning, both in the household arts and the broad base of book knowledge that his ideal of a woman would one day bring to her equally educated and deserving husband. He gave them his own love obsessively, but made them "earn" it. To Maria at age eleven, when she had a tendency to freckle, he could write an admonishment not to go out without wearing her bonnet "because it will make you very ugly and then we should not love you so much."[11] He did this to her often enough that she must have known he was not merely teasing.

She had learned French well in Europe but was a poor student of Spanish, and the whole family seemed to agonize with her as she labored through her assigned ten pages daily of *Don Quixote*. She must also learn to set a hen, cut a beefsteak, make a pudding, and thus forever merit her father's affection. It would gratify him, he once wrote her, "to see that you are improved in Spanish, in writing, in needle work, in good humor, and kind and generous dispositions; and that you grow daily more and more worthy the love of, dear Maria, Your's affectionately."[12] Martha had bent resiliently to this kind of badgering, but Maria could not. She was to become timid, introverted, and delicate, and would die in 1804 (survived by husband John Wayles Eppes and two children), still smothered in father-love while fearing paradoxically that her father did not love her enough.

Late in January, Jefferson wrote to Martha that he was alone at present, with Maria and the two grandchildren, but was hoping for a visit from his sister Anne (Mrs. Hastings Marks) soon. His weather memoranda, farm book, garden book, and account books provide ample evidence of the trivia that often filled his days. From his account book for January:

Jan. 6. Sent Price by Tom Shackleford 30/ for 12 turkies.
11. Gave Mr. Petit to bear exp. to Augusta for sheep 12/.
18. Small exp. 1/6
26. Pd for 5-3/4 lb butter @ 1/3.
27. Maria for small exp. 4/6.
31. 4 negroe men arrive, hired from Colo-

nel TMR's [Thomas Mann Randolph's] estate. They brought with them 3 mares purchasd. for me from ditto.

Jefferson and his Virginia colleagues were less involved with the improvement of livestock, which was seldom a cash product, than they were with crop betterment. Still, they practiced a rudimentary selection process for better sheep, cattle, and hogs. They seldom gave their animals winter shelter, other than crude and often temporary open sheds. At Mount Vernon, Washington was leading the way toward the use of permanent barns for livestock protection and grain storage, but Jefferson had no substantial barns comparable to Washington's.

Sheep were dual-purpose creatures, producing both wool and meat; some cattle labored in the fields and also produced milk and eventually meat; but hogs were solely for slaughter, and the fatter the better. American farmers followed the English example as expressed by agriculturist and pamphleteer William Cobbett, who believed that a hog should be so heavy that it must sit down to eat its last bushel of potatoes and bran before slaughter. With cattle, fatness to the point of obesity was less important. There was a preference for the all-purpose animal that would produce milk and butter for a few years, or serve as a draft ox in the fields, and then could be slaughtered for meat. Steers or bulls kept specifically for meat were of low quality. As Washington complained to British agriculturist Arthur Young, "We have, in a manner, everything to learn that respects neat & profitable husbandry."[13]

During the previous fall, Jefferson had owned about 250 head of cattle and 400 hogs. Since January and February were slaughtering months, the numbers were being gradually reduced, and kitchens and smokehouses were crammed with new flitches of bacon, souse, griskins, blade-bones, spare-ribs, chines, bellies, cheeks, hams, and flitches of sidemeat to be smoked for bacon. Concerning one other kind of livestock, poultry, there is little in the record. There is mention of eggs but little evidence of where they came from, except that—in earlier times when Jefferson was away—Martha had promised to visit the fowls when the weather permitted. There are other indications that the slaves raised poultry, not only for themselves but to sell, along with eggs, to the household. Jefferson's account book lists payments to Betty Hemings for pullets and hens. As the raising of exotic Bantam chickens was considered a proper hobby for young girls, Jefferson had brought three pair from France and put them in Maria's charge. "Tell me when you shall have the first chickens hatched," he used to say in his letters. "How many chickens have you raised this summer?"

January and February passed among these scenes of steaming barnyards and noisy chicken pens, the ringing of axes and the clunk of the grubbing hoes. The mail, always slow getting up from Richmond by post rider, was even slower because so few friends owed letters to Jefferson. Always fretting about the delayed mail, Jefferson had even tried giving one letter to the Orange County post rider and a duplicate to the Charlottesville–Richmond rider, to see which reached Madison in Philadelphia first. The results were inconclusive.

But Madison owed him a letter now, and on an important topic. Jefferson had written him just after Christmas, purportedly to comment upon last year's Whiskey Rebellion but with another, ingenious motive. Jefferson had felt profound resentment at the government's action against the tax-resisting farmers of western Pennsylvania, whose distilled spirits proved to be the only form in which they could market their productions, and had complained of "such an armament against people at their ploughs," and he was further hurt by the fact that the Rebellion had prompted Washington to blame the "democratic societies," voluntary organizations put together to advance an anti-Federalist viewpoint. Jefferson thought Hamilton had persuaded Washington to attack these societies in the latter's annual message to Congress.

In his letter of late December to Madison, Jefferson had said, "It is wonderful indeed, that the President should have permitted himself to be the organ of such an attack on the freedom of discussion, the freedom of writing, printing & publishing." Then he had made a bold suggestion to Madison, who was trying to hold the line for republicanism in Congress, while Jefferson had distanced himself from the battle. He had urged Madison not to consider retiring "unless to a more splendid & a more efficacious post."[14] In short, he had suggested that Madison consider the presidency. It was as if he anticipated that he might himself be asked to run in 1796 and was moving early to avoid it.

Like the plowing of fields, the spading of earth for brickmaking was tied to the weather. By the end of January, the process of brickmaking was on Jefferson's mind, and he wrote to ask Randolph what had happened to their instructions for making bricks without treading the mortar. Could Randolph get them, if he had misplaced them? He was not to start serious remodeling of the house for another year, but first a great many bricks had to be molded and fired. His preoccupation with brickmaking resulted in several lines in his farm book. He did not yet have a kiln in operation, but would have one the following year when his housebuilding was in fuller sway. Meanwhile, he had gathered some facts and figures with which to judge the progress of his brickmaking. Four cubic feet of earth made a thousand bricks, and a man could make a couple of thousand a day if he had a helper to tamp and another to cart away the bricks and stack them. Jefferson calculated that an acre of land would yield a million bricks for every foot of earth spaded.

The house as it now stood had been developed over a decade, before his assignment to Paris, and it may once have pleased him, based as it was upon the ideas of Andrea Palladio, the Italian architect whom he admired. Now, however, after his extended architectural observations abroad, he was eager to rebuild the place. His intention was to produce a single-story house with a dome—he had seen what he wanted in the Hôtel de Salm in Paris—and to double the width of the building. He was still a long way from completing the unique dependencies which, connected to the main house, permitted the busy life of the mansion to go forward without intruding upon the eye.

The month of February came and Madison showed no signs of acknowledging Jefferson's idea. In fact, the usually prompt Madison wrote no letters at all during January and February. The mundane life of a farmer dominated all. A mule that had been sent up from Varina got out of the new stable, apparently through the carelessness of Jupiter, and Jefferson asked Randolph to watch for her in case she returned home. He said he might send Jupiter after her as punishment for his error.

From Switzerland came a letter from François D'Ivernois, offering to transfer to Virginia the whole of an educational institution called the Geneva Academy, with its entire faculty. Jefferson referred the matter to the Virginia legislature and wrote to Washington about it. The matter rather conflicted with Washington's current notion of establishing a national university in the District of Columbia, supported by the income from inland navigation of the Potomac and James rivers. He was not inclined to support D'Ivernois, to whom Jefferson sent his noncommittal thanks.

Another loyal correspondent, John Adams, had written early in the month to report on changes in the executive department. Timothy Pickering was replacing Henry Knox as secretary of war; Hamilton had resigned as secretary of the treasury—perhaps with notions of advancement—to be replaced by a weak Oliver Wolcott. Edmund Randolph had become secretary of state. Said Adams, "Those Republicans who delight in Rotations will be gratified in all Probability, till all the Ablest Men in the Nation are roted out."[15]

As if apprehensive that the slightest recognition of the musical-chairs game in Philadelphia would somehow thrust his own name forward, Jefferson carefully ignored Adams's remark. Instead, he answered an earlier letter from Adams by saying, "In truth I have so much occupation otherwise that I have not time for taking a part in any thing of a public kind, and I therefore leave such with pleasure to those who are to live longer and enjoy their benefits."[16]

It was the old refrain, and not likely to deceive John Adams.

March

March always brought a flurry of gardening, and with it a spate of writing in the garden book. The previous spring, when Jefferson was newly reprieved from his bondage in government and found delight in everything having to do with the house and grounds, he had bubbled over with remarks to jot into his book. He had reported when he sowed peas, when the peas came up, and when he "sowed a second batch of the same." But now that writing was more an intrusion on his daily routine, he neglected the record he had sustained for thirty years. He made not a single entry having to do with vegetables or flowers.

Eventually the Monticello vegetable garden would extend along a one-thousand-foot terrace gouged from the side of the mountain and supported by a stone wall. It was less impressive in 1795 than later, but still was the proud attainment of an avid gardener. He carried in his memory the wondrous gardening sense of the English and French, whose homes he had visited. His large collection of books on gardening was cataloged under "Fine Arts."

At the start of the month the farm land was still too wet to plow but was drying rapidly. By the fifth, the plowmen were in the fields with horses and oxen and it was time to cut back on the odd jobs of winter. By the ninth, John Hemings and several other slaves had spaded up earth to be used that year in brickmaking, and in recent days had cut twenty-three cords of wood for the fireplaces and fifty more for Silkknitter's charcoal operation. The mules had brought in more than four hundred hampers of charcoal already burned in the outlying woodland.

Manure was being carted to the fields on both sides of the river, to be plowed under. To Jefferson and his neighbors, manure was not just a byproduct of the alimentation of cattle and sheep, but any substance added to the soil to improve it, such as

Apr. 19. two or three days of severe weather attended with frost have killed most of the
fruit in the neighborhood. here it is safe as yet, and I surmised today that it is safe as low down as the old orchard at the where the
4. fields corner together. about half the almonds however are killed
it is safer to the river, but not at Tufton.

may. 12 in clearing the road between helfields & scitfield, where there was no digging, but
every there was grubbed up which could be grubbed, & the larger trees were cut down
to a width of 1. pole, 4 men did 220. yds a day which was 10. square poles each.
I ascertained on that line the steps of my horse as a rough way of estimating
distances without getting down to stride them off. when pushed into a brisk
a walk he stepped the 220. yds at 112 steps descending & 116. steps ascending.
110 steps would have been 2. yds at a step. 114 (the medium) is 5 9/1. the step.

1802.

may 11. planted grape vines received from Legaux in the S.W. vineyard in vacant spaces from
up the upper or 1st row very large white eating grapes.
2d row } 30. plants of vines from Burgundy and champagne with roots.
3d do.
4th row } 30. plants of vines of Bordeaux with roots.
5th row
6th row. 10. plants of vines from Cape of good hope with roots.
26. planted in the upper row of the Nursery beginning at the N.E. end the fol-
-lowing peach stones, sent me by Marrei from Pisa. see his letter.
4. stones of the Maddalena peach. then 4. of the poppe de Venere. then 12 melon peaches.
then 60. Vaga loggia.
also planted a great number of Paccan nuts, in the same rows of those plan-
-ted the two last years.

1803.

Mar. 12. the well was observed about a month ago to have a plenty of water in it
after having been dry about 18. months.
my ice house here has taken 62. waggon loads of ice to fill it, have 1. foot
thickness of shavings between it and the wall all around. the whole cost
including labour, feeding, drink &c. has been 70. D.
21. peach trees begin to blossom
24. a considerable snow on the blue ridge
25. thermom. at sunrise 34°
28. thermom. at sunrise 29°

The garden activities as recorded by Jefferson in his Garden
Book. Courtesy of the Massachusetts Historical Society.

marl, plaster of Paris, pearl ash, straw, or clover turned over by the plowshare as it stood in the field.

Some crops seemed to improve the soil they were grown upon and some exhausted it, but no one knew why. The advanced farmers knew that leguminous crops such as alfalfa (then called lucerne), peas, beans, or clover would make their soil more productive, but of nitrogen and the bacteria that fixed it in the soil they were ignorant.

They knew well that tobacco was a soil-exhausting crop. Certain "unthrifty" farmers planted it year upon year, and when the soil wore out they grubbed a few more acres of vanishing woodland. Jefferson had observed that in Virginia it was cheaper to clear an acre of new land than to manure an old one. As long, that is, as there was new land available.

Not to have a cash crop like tobacco was unthinkable. Every other product of the farm was consumed on the premises by slaves and their owners, or by livestock. The cash crop was almost certainly shipped out to Europe in exchange for artifacts of the good life. The newest cash crop was wheat, and Jefferson's goal was to replace all his tobacco land with wheat and to achieve a workable crop rotation. The books on agriculture in his personal library spanned the centuries, from *Maison Rustique, or the Countrie*

Farme (London, 1600), to John Spurrier's *The Practical Farmer* (Wilmington, Delaware, 1793). What he needed now, and wrote to Philadelphia for, was "a pamphlet entitled 'Sketches on rotations of crops,' to be had I believe at Dobson's." He did not then know it was written by his friend John Beale Bordley, a prominent agriculturist.

This year was to mark his second try at a novel crop rotation, to run for seven years:

1. Wheat, followed by turnips for sheep feed.
2. Corn and potatoes, grown together, followed by vetch (a beanlike forage crop he was trying for the first time in the fall).
3. Peas or potatoes, or both.
4. Wheat or rye, sown with red clover.
5. Clover.
6. Clover, plowed under in the fall and sown to vetch.
7. Vetch turned under, buckwheat sown in spring, followed by wheat in the fall, restarting the cycle.

Although Jefferson had borrowed this seven-year rotation from Washington, it was characteristically more complicated than that of the president, who still used only five kinds of crops in his plan. As Jefferson discussed his system with one of the most knowledgeable farmers in the commonwealth, John Taylor of Caroline County, he received wise and often stern counsel. Taylor said that he, too, had started farming with a strong bias against corn but had gradually been won over to it. Corn had the advantage of producing bread, fodder, and animal manure in abundance. Turnips and potatoes, on the other hand, produced animal food only. Turnips required land in garden condition. Potatoes needed too much labor. The food and straw production of peas was scanty. Corn was the only crop Jefferson was undertaking, said Taylor, that provided a complete food for man and beast.

As if to be completely perverse, Taylor said he preferred cattle over sheep for feeding slaves. Sheep were delicate and subject to distempers; were unable to convert coarse materials into manure; and produced no milk, cheese, or butter. He claimed a cow would yield her value in manure annually, and also in milk, cheese, and butter.

It would seem strange to later generations that farmers of Jefferson's day fed potatoes, turnips, and other succulent foods to livestock. Washington was also trying squash, rutabagas, and even melons. Their nutritional value could only be guessed at by observing how sleek the animals looked and how fat they grew. Jefferson fed potatoes in a trough, chopped, with a handful of bran for relish, and he believed that two measures of potatoes yielded as much nutrition as a single measure of corn. John Taylor thought that potatoes were good for horses and cattle, but said his sheep would scarcely eat them and his hogs would gorge upon them until they died. (No doubt the cattle and sheep, as ruminants, could convert some of the cellulose into protein, but it is difficult to imagine horses thriving on such low-protein foods.)

Another aspect of agriculture in which Jefferson and his colleagues on the farms sought improvement was in crop variety. Washington raised or attempted to raise more than sixty species or varieties of plants. Farmers tinkered with such crops as chicory, Guinea grass, hop clover, sainfoin, Jerusalem artichoke, horse beans, burnet, and Siberian melilot. Jefferson brought back cuttings of olive trees from Italy and southern France in the hope that Americans would find them a profitable source of oil. He sought out rice that would flourish in dry fields, hoping that South Carolinians could raise rice on upland soils and escape the miasmas, fevers and agues he attributed to standing water.

During the last week of March, Jefferson sowed red clover seed. At his request, John Taylor had built him a "seed box" or drill for faster and more consistent planting. It is no surprise that Jefferson, the lover of gadgets, was the first to try new kinds of farm machinery. He was in the process of developing a more efficient moldboard (the adjunct to a plowshare that flips the sod over), but it would not be ready to try for another year. Using mathematical principles, he had designed it for manufacture in any farmer's workshop, and wanted no patent on it. As secretary of state he had been in charge of the patent office, and had issued a patent to Eli Whitney for a cotton gin, but his own preference was to put his improvements into the public domain for unrestricted use.

March was the time to bottle the cider that had been laid up in casks in the fall. Like wine, cider would not wait. The household servants attended to the bottling off, with Jupiter or Ursula supervising, no doubt counting the usable bottles and corks anxiously, for they always seemed to be in short supply. Jefferson ordered both from England, one order specifying six gross of corks for use with wine, cider, and apple vinegar.

Cider of about 7 percent alcohol was as much a

staple of the early American diet as was beer, until its widespread use was suppressed by the temperance movement of the nineteenth century. There was connoisseurship in cider; Jefferson judged it as he judged fine wines. If it had to be drunk before it was fit, a grating of ginger would render it bearable. The best was made from the fruits of the Monticello orchard, but often if the season was bad Jefferson tried to buy it in the cask from notable cider regions such as Suffolk or Smithfield.

The lore of cidermaking was deeply ingrained. Jefferson thought the best apples were Taliaferro (pronounced "Tolliver") and Red Hughes. Poor apples with wormy or bruised spots were not to be used, for the fruit must be immaculate, worked over by hand before being crushed into pomace and the juice pressed out. Carefully nursed through the winter, the tart-sweet fluid became to Jefferson "more like wine than any liquor I have ever tasted which was not wine."[17]

Two years before, there had been a debacle in the cider cellar while he was on the job in Philadelphia. Martha had written him in the summer of 1793:

I have a terible account to give you of your cyder. Of 140 bottles that were put away you will hardly find 12. It flew in such a manner as to render it dangerous going near them. Those that were carelessly corked forced their corks, the rest burst the bottles amongst which the havoc is incredible.[18]

That was to Jefferson part of the price he had paid for years of absence from household and field.

Near the end of March the long-awaited letter from Madison arrived. Jefferson's old friend slammed the door gently, almost softly, on any suggestion that he might allow his own name to be put forward for the presidency. With judicious underscoring of words, he made his point "that reasons of *every* kind, and some of them, of the most *insuperable* as well as *obvious* kind, shut my mind against the admission of any idea such as you seem to glance at."

Historian Dumas Malone comments upon the obliqueness of language which "reflected their un-voiced feeling that this office should not be directly sought—least of all by a gentleman reared in the Vir-ginia tradition."[19] One could "stand" for office, meaning he could hold still for it, but he should not run for it.

Yet Madison saw no harm in teasing with an obscurely subtle reference to Jefferson's standing for the office himself. He put it this way: "You ought to be preparing yourself however to hear truths, which no inflexibility will be able to withstand."[20] Going into his second year of retirement, with so many things blossoming, and pale green rows of peas now bursting upon the garden, Jefferson could enjoy the wordplay but still reject the idea.

April and May

The month of April was rather early for a crop failure in Virginia, except for Jefferson's favorite crop, peaches. This year, two or three days of bad weather including frost kept him apprehensive for several days.

His orchard at this time was mainly on the southeastern slope, below the house, and some of it extended far enough into the river valley to be vulnerable to the frosts that always struck the low places where cold air settled. A difference of a few feet in elevation could be crucial. The apples were tough enough to survive most frosts, but his peaches and apricots were not. This time he was lucky and the crop survived.

Almost none of Jefferson's fruit trees were native to North America; his ancestors had brought their love of fruits from England and Europe. Many trees found their way to Europe from the Orient and came to American shores with the first colonists. Jefferson called his fruit "that precious refreshment," and tried to raise as much as possible, even the delicate Seville oranges that needed indoor shelter in winter. His cherries included the Carnation ("so superior to all others that no other deserves the name of cherry"), Ox Heart, Duke, and Morello.[21] His plums bore names still familiar: Green Gage, Brignole, Prune-Plum, and Damson (he wrote the name uncontracted, "Damascene"). Pears included the Seckel, English, Richmond, and Beurré.

Jefferson's devotion to apples went beyond his craving for cider; it was almost a cultural trait. By 1686, William Fitzhugh of Westmoreland County was said to have had an orchard of twenty-five hundred trees. At Monticello the varieties included the Esopus Spitzenburgh (nine years to produce fruit); Newtown Pippin, a good keeper that later would be known as the Albemarle Pippin; Golden Wilding; Codling; Pearmain; Mammoth; Pumgray; and Sunbriar.

Jefferson's delight in the peach tree was far more complex than his attention to apples and other fruits, for he was unusually fond of both the fresh fruit and the distilled brandy. He took new hope in springtime from the blossoming peaches of April, and devised ingenious ways to use the trees—and even their dead wood—at Monticello.

In France, he had observed that French pears and apricots were superior to those in America, but not the peaches. The Spanish had brought them to Mexico and Florida long before the British settlements had appeared, and their cultivation by Indians had led settlers to suppose that they were native fruits. He wrote to a friend that "tho' we graft all other kinds of fruits, we rarely graft the peach, the nectarine, the apricot or the almond. The tree proceeding from the stone yields a faithful copy of its fruit, & the tree is always healthier."[22] Not so with apples, cherries, or plums, which seldom reproduced faithfully from seed, so that to continue a desirable variety it was necessary to graft twigs or buds from a parent tree to a new, young one. Jefferson was adept at grafting and budding, both called "inoculating," and had first mentioned the name of his famed homesite in his garden book for 1767, when he wrote that he had "inoculated common cherry buds into stocks of large kind at Monticello."[23]

Jefferson's love for the peach led him to try thirty-seven varieties during his lifetime. "I am endeavoring to make a collection of the choicest kinds of peaches for Monticello."[24] If numbers are an indication, his favorite might have been the October clingstone; he once instructed his overseer to plant five hundred of them in his nursery and secure them safely against rabbits by a close fence made of palings. For flavor, he could have chosen the Portugal, of which, in sending a pint of stones to George Mason, he said that, if well tended, they produced the finest fruit he ever tasted. For old times' sake, however, he might have singled out the plum peach, apparently the first fruit he had grown at Monticello in 1769. Other favorites were the Oldmixon freestone and clingstone; the Mammoth or Early Chelmsford, ripening by the end of August; the lemon peach, a hardy clingstone; the Blood clingstone, with a purplish skin and deep red flesh, very good in cooking; and the Green Nutmeg or Early Anne, a small white peach from England. The Alberge, a winter clingstone, seemed useful only for making preserves.

Because peach trees tend to produce many dead limbs that must be trimmed away, Jefferson asked Tom Randolph to help him calculate how many trees it would take to furnish dead wood for his fireplaces. He figured that five acres of trimmable trees would feed one fireplace throughout the winter. To keep ten fireplaces aglow, he thought he might plant a large, circular plot of peaches partially embracing the mansion grounds, from a hundred to three hundred yards from the house, close enough that the slaves might carry in the wood without needing a cart.

As he disliked cutting down a living tree, even for badly needed firewood, he had thought to produce another kind of wood as an ongoing crop. He had planted in the previous year eleven hundred shoots of the weeping willow, a very fast-growing tree. He estimated that if eight willows would yield a cord of wood each time they were lopped off, and could stand to be lopped every third year, then eight hundred trees would yield one hundred cords of wood a year. The experiment appears to have lapsed.

To simplify his seven-year crop rotation scheme, Jefferson had divided each of his four farms near Monticello into seven fields of forty acres each. Instead of fencing these fields with rails or by other means, he had decided to mark them simply with rows of peach trees. To achieve this end, he had planted in December more than eleven hundred small trees along the dividing lines. Within a year or

In his diary for 1795, Jefferson monitored the progress of the farms and crops. Courtesy of the Massachusetts Historical Society.

so, when he wrote "peach trees begin to blossom" in his garden book, it would denote a beautiful neighborhood occurrence.

Other farm work was proceeding. Manure was hauled, corn planting began, and buckwheat—a new crop with him—was sown on land that he would plant to regular wheat in the fall after plowing the buckwheat under to improve the soil.

The mail was sparse, both incoming and outgoing, but toward the end of April Jefferson wrote two letters worth noting. That his isolation was beginning to chafe is shown in his remarks to Virginia Senator William Branch Giles: "I shall be rendered very happy by the visit you promise me. The only thing wanting to make me completely so, is the more frequent society of my friends. It is the more wanting, as I am becoming more firmly fixed to the globe."[25]

His letter to Madison was mainly a response to the startling suggestion that he should prepare to be put up as a candidate for the presidency in the following year. He confessed that standing for this office (he could not bring himself to name it) had crossed his mind, but the reasons he had put forth for his resignation from the secretaryship were even more valid as arguments against a higher office. He used two of his stock reasons, both of which must have seemed threadbare to Madison. He was now committed to the land, he explained, and his health had utterly broken down during the last eight months. It is true that he had suffered a serious attack of joint inflammation the previous summer, but there were no other indications of ruinous health problems.

"My age requires that I should place my affairs in a clear state," he wrote. "The question is forever closed with me." He was then fifty-two and would live another thirty-one years.

Then some small talk:

> I am proceeding in my agricultural plans with a slow but sure step. To get under full way will require 4. or 5. years. . . . My little essay in red clover, the last year, has had the most encouraging success. . . . I have sowed this year about 120. [acres] which the rain now falling comes very opportunely on.[26]

He told Madison that in May he would visit his other Virginia location, Poplar Forest in Bedford County, but there is no record that he did so. Poplar Forest was his collective term for three properties, still comprising a kind of agricultural outpost of his principal lands around Monticello. Although he had not yet built his interesting octagonal house on the property, he often went there in summer to relax, and in 1781 he had stayed there while writing part of his only published book, *Notes on the State of Virginia.* His wife had inherited the tract of about five thousand acres from her father, of which about eight hundred acres were in cultivation. Every fall, his Poplar Forest overseer or a reliable servant led a caravan of wagons and livestock from there to Monticello, transporting tobacco and other farm crops, beeves and fat hogs, dried fruits, and butter salted down for the winter.

Madison is said to have visited Monticello at about that time with his bride of a few months, Dolley Payne Todd. The visit may have coincided with the day the garden peas were ready for the table, as there was a tradition among Madison, Jefferson, and George Divers of nearby Farmington that the first to get a mess of new peas would give a dinner for the other two. "New peas come to table" was a common entry in the garden book.

Farming operations continued with the planting of potatoes, cutting the first crop of red clover, cultivating corn, and bringing in strawberries and Early May Duke cherries from garden and orchard, all such events duly recorded in the garden and farm books.

And then there was the nailery. Home industries were common among the farmers of Virginia: George Washington sold the products of his fishery, distillery, and weaving shop, and Jefferson could by May of the current year consider that his new nail factory was in full production. "What with my farming and my nail manufactory," he wrote John Adams, "I have my hands full. I am on horseback half the day, and counting and measuring nails the other half."[27]

He had begun to work on the nailery more than a year earlier, making it a part of his blacksmith shop (another small industry) on Mulberry Row. Apparently he had hit upon the idea because of its low capital needs. He could put slave boys to work there before they were sturdy enough to labor in the fields, and there was always a market for nails in a heavily settled area. It is fascinating, almost unsettling, to read of Jefferson the violinist, Latinist, wine fancier, and framer of the Declaration delighting in the glowing fires of a forge and the clink of new nails as the nail-cutting machine chopped and shaped them.

He brought nailrod from Philadelphia via Richmond, and began his operation with a single charcoal fire. As the enterprise began to get on its feet, he made up cards showing nails of different kinds and sizes, and sent them out to merchants in Albemarle,

Augusta, and adjacent counties, and in Richmond. By midsummer he would be making from eight to ten thousand nails a day and feeling proud of the undertaking. To Jean-Nicholas Démeunier, in France, he wrote: "My new trade of nail-making is to me in this country what an additional title of nobility or the ensigns of a new order are in Europe."[28]

Another home industry that had been lagging for years may have returned to Jefferson's attention when he received a new book by Oliver Evans. The prominent inventor of steam engines and other machinery had just published *The Young Mill-Wright & Miller's Guide* (Philadelphia, 1795), with Jefferson and Washington listed in the back as subscribers. The mill at Shadwell that Jefferson had inherited from his father had long ago washed away in a "fresh." Now he was planning to build another one, perhaps two, near the old site. He envisioned a canal to divert water from the Rivanna for this purpose. The Rivanna, also called the north fork of the James, was essential to the commerce of Jefferson's region, and as a young farmer thirty years earlier he had helped to clear a channel for barges traveling to and from Richmond.

A year that had begun poorly, with inclement weather retarding the farming and threatening the orchards, had straightened itself out by the end of May, although the wheat crop promised to be poor. To Adams, Jefferson wrote:

> We have had a hard winter and backward spring . . . strawberries not ripe till within this fortnight, and every thing backward in proportion. . . . I am trying potatoes on a large scale as a substitute for Indian corn for feeding animals. This is new in this country, but in this culture we cannot rival you.[29]

June and July

The hot and sticky season was well begun, and the field hands were going through the corn with hoes. Perhaps during one of his daily rides to the farms on both sides of the river, Jefferson decided that he wanted another mechanical contrivance to toy with. He wrote to General Henry Knox of Massachusetts, just retired as secretary of war, about a wind-powered machine:

> I recollect you were so kind as to undertake to give me an account of the success of an experiment made at Boston with a mill

. . . to go with either wind or water. The axis was vertical. The sails were in frames like doors. . . . I want much to erect something which may work as a saw mill, or work a smith's smiting hammer in a place where I can have no agent but wind.[30]

The place was Mulberry Row, where the blacksmith shop and nailery were located. No such windmill was ever built.

The next six weeks were to be filled with pure agriculture and the daily decisions of a country gentleman. Maria and the grandchildren were with him, and numerous ailing relatives and friends were to find their way to him later. A family sadness and a disturbing event in government were to occupy his thoughts before the end of July.

When barley ripened on the old Shadwell farm, the hands swarmed over it with cradle and scythe. Barley was an animal feed which Jefferson seldom mentioned, and it was not a regular part of his crop rotation, but it was an ingredient of beer and hard liquor. With a distillery in mind, Jefferson may have begun to experiment with the manufacture of spirits. But wheat was the big operation. Even the nailery fires were quenched so that every child and healthy adult could join the platoon of reapers, cradlers, stackers, and gatherers. The farm book shows that the usually pampered household servants were among the gatherers.

In the farm book, Jefferson recorded his harvest plan for the next year and concluded that a really well run wheat operation would require sixty-six field hands, including a man to drive a cart from tree to tree where the workers gathered to rest, with a cask of liquor to refresh them. He estimated the gallons of liquor required as he might figure the bushels of potatoes needed to sustain a team of oxen.

From John Breckenridge, a migrant to the lush grasslands of Kentucky, came a letter enclosing some clover seed that Jefferson had requested. To his old friend, Breckenridge could not resist adding that he wished he could send some Kentucky soil also. "I fear the seed will not acknowledge that about Monticello. I sincerely wish 1000 of the tens of thousand of acres of our fertile uncultivated land, could be spread around you."[31]

When enough wheat had been stacked to start the treading operation, the treading floor was laid near the storage bins. This primitive method of separating grain from straw was so unsatisfactory that Jefferson was determined to have one of the new

71

threshing machines from Scotland as soon as possible. Even that machine required horse power, the
horses walking in a circle to turn the moving parts of
the contrivance, but it was not nearly so hard on the
animals as the endless treading down of knee-high
piles of wheat so that their hooves could grind and
chop the grain away from the straw.

At the house sickness had affected Jefferson's
three visiting sisters and several other persons not
identified. Maria helped to nurse them until she also
fell ill. Jefferson's account book for July shows a
paper transaction of $40.00 involving Dr. William
Wardlaw, of Charlottesville, which may have covered house calls during this uneasy period.

Martha Randolph and her husband passed through
on their way from Varina to the Warm Springs, across
the Blue Ridge, in the hope that Tom might experience a change of health. He was a mercurial, often
tempestuous man, never at peace, and his ills were
recognized by Jefferson as emotional and his situ-
ation virtually "hopeless." He rode like a Cossack to
slake his inner anger, and would one day be captain
of a company of militia cavalry. He had been to New
York and Boston in search of medical help. Now he
turned to the classic treatment of the times: go to the
springs and take the waters.

The Tea Room was a place to entertain guests and seek repose. It is a semi-octagonal projection off the northern end of the Dining Room. Jefferson called this his "most honorable suite" because he kept the likenesses of many American heroes on display here. Courtesy of the Thomas Jefferson Memorial Foundation, Inc. (photograph by James Tkatch).

During the period of malaise at Monticello, word came that the Randolphs' infant child had died. Jefferson sent James Hemings to Staunton for the body, and there Alexander Stuart decided to send another man to accompany the tiny corpse home in a carriage, the Randolphs staying on to continue Tom's treatments. The account book shows a payment of $6.00 to Stuart's carriage driver for bringing "dear little Eleanora," and on the same day, Benjamin Snead was paid $2.00 for reading a service over the child as she was interred in the family burial plot.

Apparently there was concern in the family that the long trip from Varina to the Warm Springs had contributed to the death of the child. Jefferson tried to comfort the parents in his letter of July 28: "It is great consolation to us that your stay at Staunton had been so long as to render it impossible that the journey could have had any effect on the accident which happened." He said that his sisters Mary Bolling, Martha Carr, and Anne Marks all were indisposed, and also Mary's daughter Polly and their two servants.[32]

Another distraction at this disturbing time brought Jefferson's thoughts sharply back to the national scene and even stirred him to acerbic comment about the trend of government. Jefferson's friends in

Philadelphia knew, because he certainly had told them emphatically, that he was rusticating without ever seeing a Philadelphia newspaper. Now and then he apparently received a clipping, or a single copy, from Madison and others who had a motive for keeping him abreast of the times. So it happened that on July 21 Jefferson received a letter from Virginia Senator Henry Tazewell, containing an electrifying revelation published in the *Aurora*.

Benjamin Franklin's grandson, B.F. Bache, trained as a printer and publisher by his grandfather, had turned the *Aurora* into a newspaper for anti-Federalists. John Jay's treaty with Great Britain, which had been kept out of the press until after the Senate had approved it, had been slipped to Bache by another senator and immediately published. Although there was widespread disapproval of the treaty, it had been signed by Washington in good conscience, as an alternative to war with England, and ratified by a two-thirds vote in the Senate.

Chief Justice Jay had been sent as a minister plenipotentiary to arrange the treaty in the midst of the war going on between Great Britain and France, and in which the United States hoped not to become entangled. Jefferson had feared that Hamilton might be sent, and could not understand why, in any case, the regular minister Thomas Pinckney could not be given the assignment. Not the best possible choice, Jay had been outclassed by the British negotiators and come home with a treaty which was, to the Jeffersonians, greatly flawed.

The document had grown out of the Treaty of Peace of 1783, which had ended the Revolution but left some neutral rights unclear and created some trade complications. The Jay agreement removed some dilemmas while creating others, and was an obvious victory for the Federalists and Jefferson's old foe, Alexander Hamilton. The British promised to clear out of certain military posts in the Old Northwest. The United States could trade with the West Indies, but on disadvantageous terms. Nothing was done about vexatious British impressment of American sailors. And Britain was given an advantage over France in commercial matters. It was the kind of treaty that was, on first reading, truly outrageous. Samuel Flagg Bemis, analyzing it a century and a half later, saw it as essential in regaining American "territorial integrity" in the Northwest, and in keeping the peace with Great Britain. Other modern historians have praised Washington for having taken the long view and easing the treaty through Congress.

By the time Jefferson got the *Aurora* announcement, a month had passed since the Senate had approved the treaty, but it had yet to be signed by the president or by the British, who would have to consider a provision eliminated by Congress. It was too late for Jefferson's voice to be effective—he had created that circumstance for himself by retiring— but he showed his frustration and anger in letters to his friends.

To Tazewell he wrote that knuckling under to insult is not the way to escape war:

> Tho I have interdicted myself all serious attention to political matters, yet a very slight notice of that in question sufficed to decide my mind against it. I am not satisfied we should not be better without treaties with any nation. But I am satisfied we should be better without such as this.[33]

In a sense he may have been blaming himself for having left the conflict to men less adept than he was. To Mann Page he wrote: "They say that while all hands were below deck mending sails, splicing ropes, and every one at his own business, & the captain in his cabbin attending to his log book & chart, a rogue of a pilot has run them into an enemy's port."[34] In this apt metaphor, the crafty pilot at the wheel may not have been Jay, but Jefferson's old nemesis Alexander Hamilton.

During the summer, another treaty negotiation more to Jefferson's liking was being negotiated on the frontier. The United States Army under command of General Anthony Wayne had defeated a formidable, British-influenced force of Indians at the Battle of Fallen Timbers in the Ohio River Valley. Later, after three days of feasting and drinking at Greenville, Indians representing all the tribes between the Great Lakes and the Mississippi River ceded a large portion of the Northwest Territory and, everyone hoped, ended two decades of fighting on that frontier.

Jefferson could not have realized how the negotiations at Greenville would dominate his later public life. Because of that treaty, breaking the combined resistance of strong tribes east of the Mississippi, the way was cleared for unlimited westward expansion. Jefferson was to become a kind of superintendent of that expansion, through his role in the Louisiana Purchase and the expeditions of Lewis and Clark and other explorers. Present at the treaty grounds were two young army officers also unaware of their destiny, Meriwether Lewis and William Clark.

August and September

The chronicler who finds the month of August a near blank is likely to feel more tolerant of Sarah Randolph's declaration that the year 1795 was a zero in Jefferson's life. August in Virginia can be so torrid and damp that a traveler to the Blue Ridge, seeking comfort at the crest of Old Rag or even the Peaks of Otter, senses little difference between the mountaintop and the sweltering banks of the Rivanna. The corn is tasseling, the wheat nearly harvested, the roadsides turned sere. The fall harvest of autumn produce is beginning; the grapes at the woods' edge are inclining toward purple.

This August was memorable in Jefferson's neighborhood for what it did to his corn crop. Rains came endlessly, wreaking temporary damage to his year's crop and permanent injury to his farms through erosion. He complained in a letter to Martha and Tom Randolph that the corn had all been so bent over by the torrents that he doubted if the tassels could drop enough pollen onto the ears to fertilize them properly. The tobacco had "fired," or sunburned, so much that neighboring farmers were harvesting theirs while it was still green. Jefferson dreaded hearing from the overseer at Bedford, where most of his tobacco was growing. As for the soil loss, he reckoned it the equivalent of a year's profit on the farms.

It would not have been a good time to remind Jefferson the agrarian of one of his most famous assertions:

Those who labour in the earth are the chosen people of God, if ever he had a chosen people, whose breasts he has made his peculiar deposit for substantial and genuine virtue. It is the focus in which he keeps alive that sacred fire, which otherwise might escape from the face of the earth.[35]

This year the sacred fire was an inferno that devoured maturing tobacco, dried up the stream beds, scorched the hay in the fields.

His correspondence was scant in August, but at the end of the month he penned a letter to Mann Page that played on some of his now-familiar themes: old age and failing health, the awful state of the world. He bewailed his failing powers in words that were more picturesque than some of his earlier self-pitying cries. "I have laid up my Rosinante in his stall, before his unfitness for the road shall expose him faultering to the world." But that was merely his excuse for not having ridden to Fredericksburg and visited Page, who had served with him in the Virginia legislature and the Continental Congress. Then he took a swipe at sculduggery everywhere:

> I do not believe with the Rochefoucaults & Montaignes, that fourteen out of fifteen men are rogues: I believe a great abatement from that proportion may be made in favor of general honesty. But I have always found that rogues would be uppermost, and I do not know that the proportion is too strong.[36]

Friends and family reaped the benefits of Jefferson's garden and wine experiments, served in the Monticello dining room. Courtesy of the Thomas Jefferson Memorial Foundation, Inc. (photograph by James Tkatch).

If there was a pleasant interlude in view, it was the turning of the grapes. Jefferson had become a wine lover long before he became a vintner, but had relied upon imports in casks and bottles to supply his needs. It was not until the arrival of Philip Mazzei, an Italian who came to Albemarle County in 1773 to start a vineyard, that Jefferson had begun to take an interest in Italian-style gardening and viniculture. He even gave Italian names to his vegetables in his garden book for 1774: *radicchio, cipolle bianche, salvastrella, prezzemolo, carote,* and *spinaci.* He began to plant Italian and French vines then, and continued even when Mazzei's plans for a winery failed.

His French period followed, with a heightened interest in French wines. He was beginning to realize, though, that Old World vines were going to be slow in adapting to New World soils and climate. When the embargo on European imports brought domestic wines to the forefront in 1808, Jefferson and his fellow connoisseurs in America turned of necessity to domestic vintages and found them bearable. By 1811 he would be writing to John Dortie:

Wine being among the earliest luxuries in which we indulge ourselves, it is desirable it should be made here and we have every soil,

aspect & climate of the best wine countries,
and I have myself drank wines made in this
state & in Maryland, of the quality of the best
Burgundy.[37]

In his declining years he would retain his taste for the
French wines he had always loved so much, but
would also be promoting the Scuppernong grape of
the Carolinas.

Earlier in the year he had received two letters
from Maria Cosway, the woman who ranked first
after his daughters on the limited roster of women
who held a firm place in his heart. He waited until
September to write her.

Mrs. Richard Cosway, an artist and musician, and
wife of an artist, had been a favorite member of the
coterie with which Jefferson had associated himself
in Paris. She had taken him unawares with talent, a
gentle charm, and a kind of coquetry against which,
as a widower still young, he had no immunity. She
had been twenty-seven and slender when they met,
with blonde hair, violet eyes, and a beautiful singing
voice. When they had parted in France, Jefferson had
written her his famed dialogue between head and
heart that is seldom passed over by his biographers:

> I am indeed the most wretched of all earthly
> beings. Overwhelmed with grief, every fibre
> of my frame distended beyond it's natural
> powers to bear, I would willingly meet what-
> ever catastrophe should leave me no more to
> feel or to fear.[38]

It was the hyperbole of infatuation, if not love,
and it surely sounds like love. As Dumas Malone
views it, "Like other deep intimacies of his life, this
one remains obscure and mysterious. Not the least
significant aspect of it is the beauty with which he
garbed the relationship in his own memory."[39]

When she wrote him in the fall of 1794, Maria
Cosway had gone into a convent and seemed anx-
ious that he should have news of her. His reply was
written on September 8; the years dimmed his ardor
to write great lines to her, although he managed to
declare "you have the power of making fair weather
wherever you go." He mainly wrote of farming:

> I am become, for instance, a real farmer,
> measuring fields, following my ploughs, help-
> ing the haymakers, and never knowing a day
> which has not done something for futurity.
> How better this, than to be shut up in the four

walls of an office, the sun ever excluded, the balmy breeze never felt, the evening closed with the barren consolation that the drudgery of the day is got through, the morning opening with the fable repeated of the Augean stable, a new load of labours in place of the old, and thus day after day worn through with no prospect before us but of more days to wear through in the same way.

But Maria Cosway still could bring poetry out of a head that teemed with thoughts of field and fold:

I had but to . . . walk out into the sun myself, tell him he does not shine on a being whose happiness I wish more than yours, pray him devoutly to bind his beams together with ten fold force, to penetrate if possible the mass of smoke and fog under which you are buried and to gild with his rays the room you inhabit and the road you travel, then tell you I have a most cordial friendship for you, that I regret the distance which separates us and will not permit myself to believe we are no more to meet till you meet me where time and distance are nothing.[40]

As the month ended, Jefferson turned his eyes toward the near shore of a personal Rubicon, the crossing of which had begun to seem thinkable if not imperative. Perhaps in a paroxysm of guilt, he wrote James Madison about a collection of pamphlets he had been receiving from the Federalist presses of Philadelphia. He had recognized the style and substance of Hamilton in pieces signed with the pseudonyms Curtius and Camillus:

> Hamilton is really a colossus to the antirepublican party. Without numbers, he is an host within himself. They have got themselves into a defile, where they might be finished; but too much security on the republican part will give time to his talents & indefatigableness to extricate them. We have had only middling performances to oppose to him. In truth, when he comes forward, there is nobody but yourself who can meet him.

The Jay treaty still rankled. "For it certainly is an attempt of a party, which finds they have lost their majority in one branch of the Legislature, to make a law by the aid of the other branch & of the executive, under color of a treaty. . . ." He had said as much before, but perhaps not so urgently. "For god's sake take up your pen, and give a fundamental reply to Curtius & Camillus."[41] He left the obvious unsaid: if Madison failed to do it, he might have to set his own pen to the task and so declare himself back in the fray.

October

C orn and wheat filled the granaries, a new planting of winter wheat was in the ground, newly
dug potatoes were piled up in the carts, and nearer
the house the making of cider and a slurry of peach
pulp and juice called *mobby* proceeded.

George Washington wrote a letter about farming
matters, avoiding comment on the turn of national affairs that had begun to separate them. He was glad
to learn that Jefferson had a good report to make on
chicory. He lamented the ways of overseers, who
would raise nothing but corn if not carefully watched.
The Albany field pea, from Europe, had not lived up

to his expectations. Neither had buckwheat, used as green manure.

> But of all the improving and ameliorating crops, none, in my opinion, is equal to Potatoes on stiff, and hard bound land (as mine is). ... In *no* instance have I failed of good wheat, Oats, or clover that followed Potatoes. And I conceit they give the soil a darker hue.

The storms of summer that had devastated Albemarle County farmland had done as much to his own at Mount Vernon. "The Rains have been very general, and more abundant since the first of August than ever happened in a summer within the memory of man."[42]

News arrived during the month that the Treaty of San Lorenzo had been negotiated with Spain. It was to bear the name of Thomas Pinckney, although it was the fruit of Jefferson's long effort to settle some prickly matters with the country that was still a threat to peace on the western frontiers. It passed the Senate unanimously, although Jefferson complained that it had not gained enough concessions. Its important provisions were the right of free navigation of the Mississippi by western settlers, although Spain still controlled the mouth of that river; and the right to deposit goods at New Orleans. The irony of the treaty negotiations was that, in their final stages, they were carried out by Federalists whose interests were not deeply involved.

On the first Tuesday in October a baby girl was born to a slave, and Jefferson entered the birth in his farm book where he kept the records of all his chattels. Christened Harriet, she was to live two years, but the fact that she was Sally Hemings's daughter would give her a kind of unhappy immortality throughout the next two centuries, and possibly beyond.

Sally, the fourteen-year-old sent to Europe with Maria, was now a woman in her early twenties, tall and straight-haired, light-skinned, and in the eyes of white men very comely. The baby was the first of her several children, born to fathers both white and black. That the Hemings matriarchy was well thought of by the Jefferson family made the children and grandchildren more conspicuous than other slaves in the Monticello neighborhood. Add the facts that miscegenation did exist in the South; that men of such probity as George Washington were falsely but commonly believed to engage in it; and that Sally and her children were all but white in appearance, and it is little wonder that Jefferson's opponents would eventually produce a story conferring on him the paternity of those children.

The first purveyor of the tale was James T. Callender, a journalist and pamphleteer whose anti-Federalist invective attracted Jefferson's attention. As Jefferson did not mind seeing scurrility turned upon his opposition now and then, he paid Callender for some unsavory writings. As his old comrade and mentor Benjamin Franklin might have said, he who lies down with dogs gets up with fleas. By 1801, for a number of reasons, Callender had turned his vituperative rage upon Jefferson.

Switching his allegiance to a Federalist newspaper in Richmond, the man began to publish various charges, including the claim that Jefferson had made Sally Hemings his concubine and fathered her children. Some of Callender's venom came in rhyme. One bland example in ballad stanzas began:

> Of all the damsels on the green,
> On mountain, or in valley,
> A lass so luscious ne'er was seen,
> As the Monticellian Sally.

It got worse, and even after Callender drowned in the James River in 1803, the engine he had created roared on. William Cullen Bryant, a thirteen-year-old lad with a talent for poetry, tried his precocious hand ("And sink supinely in her sable arms"), and by 1832 Mrs. Frances Trollope would write in *Domestic Manners of the Americans* that Jefferson was said to have fathered children "by almost all his numerous gang of female slaves."[43]

During the Civil War period, abolitionists delighted in an embellished version that had Jefferson selling his own black progeny at the auction block. Frederick Douglass, an ex-slave and black leader, claimed that one of Jefferson's granddaughters was among those free blacks who had gone to Liberia.

In 1873 the tales were revived when Madison Hemings, Sally's son, lent his name to a memoir published in an Ohio newspaper contending that Jefferson had been the father of some of Sally's children. The story was presented in English that seemed more likely the product of a country editor than a self-educated ex-slave.

The late Professor Fawn Brodie came forward with the story once more in her *Thomas Jefferson: An Intimate History*. With a book club contract and with help from eager but naive media, she brought the techniques of psychohistory, still an experimental approach, to a large audience. Professor Brodie accepted the old Callender claim and went on from

In Thomas Jefferson's bedroom, the alcove bed is open on both sides. Above the bed is a clothes closet ventilated by three oval openings in the wall. Jefferson died in this bed on July 4, 1826, the 50th anniversary of the signing of the Declaration of Independence. Courtesy of the Thomas Jefferson Memorial Foundation, Inc. (photograph by James Tkatch).

there. Her colleagues in the profession were to accuse her of using such tools as manipulation of evidence, the clever transmutation of conjecture into apparent fact, and, in too many instances, a careless reading of the record.

Recognized students of Jefferson today dissociate themselves from the Brodie canon. Those who are still interested at all may name one or the other of Jefferson's nephews, Peter and Samuel Carr, as the most likely fathers of Sally's mulatto children. The two young men were the sons of Dabney Carr, Jefferson's brother-in-law, and spent many months of their lives at or near Monticello. Originally they were identified as the miscreants by Jeffy, when grown to manhood, and speaking not from the recollections of a child but from the knowledge of one who had known Monticello life intimately and had taken charge of the place in Jefferson's last years.

Contradicting Professor Brodie's statement that the Carr brothers had left the Monticello area when Sally became pregnant, we have these entries in Jefferson's account book made early in the year, at about the time baby Harriet was conceived:

Feb. 11. Gave S. Carr to Pay Clarkson &c.
knitting 2 pr stockgs., 2 Dollars.

Mar 2. Gave P. Carr to send by S. Carr to
Dabney Carr 8 Dollars.

When the Brodie book appeared, there was some
consternation among historians, and a novel based
mainly on the Brodie speculations was declared
regrettable. But reviewer Edward Weeks may have
spoken for most reflective readers when he asked in
the *Atlantic,* "Does it really matter?"[44]

November and December

Had Jefferson kept a diary, even one so perfunctory and lackluster as Washington's lifelong "remarks & occurrences," we should have more to feed posterity's curiosity about his home life. As it is, we must cull his letters in a year when he wrote so few, and other such records as the recollections of family and slaves, to learn that he disdained foxhunting but loved to stalk squirrels and grouse, was a clever locksmith, and kept French sheepdogs descended from a bitch named Bergere that he had brought from Europe.

November was a time of battening down. The fig

trees had to be wrapped with something that Jefferson called straw rope. The ice house would be put in good repair if he had one by then; he was later to have two, one at the house to be filled with compacted snow, and another down by the river to receive real ice. How else to use the ice cream recipe he had copied down in France?

The account book entries went faithfully on. He paid his joiner David Watson 28 1/2 shillings for his latest stint. He went to Charlottesville and frittered away a shilling and a half. A doctor named Johnson paid a nail bill of 11 pounds.

The world outside was heard from again when the French writer, Constantin François, Comte de Volney, whom Jefferson had known in France, wrote to say he would like to visit Monticello during the coming June. Very well, his willing host replied, but some reconstruction would be going on. "The noise, confusion and discomfort of the scene will require all philosophy and patience."[45] The published result of Volney's visit to America was *Tableau du Climat et du Sol des États-Unis d'Amérique,* in which he described his stay at Monticello.

As the Christmas season approached, it must have seemed to his family that Jefferson had given them the finest gift by resigning from office. For the

Friends and family visiting Monticello were formally greeted in the entrance hall. Referred to as the "museum," it contained eighteen paintings and pieces of statuary, mammal bones, Indian antiquities and curiosities from the Lewis and Clark Expedition. Courtesy of the Thomas Jefferson Memorial Foundation, Inc. (photograph by James Tkatch).

second year in a row, he would be home for Christmas. Those occasions were rare in his life; usually he was on the job, sometimes actually on the road. During one period, including his years abroad, from 1774 to 1789, he spent not a single Christmas at Monticello.

Gift giving is rarely mentioned in the Jefferson records. Once Maria wrote that she had given Martha *Tales of the Castle,* by the Countess de Genlis, and that Martha had given her a small ivory box, a drawing she had made, and *The Observer,* a collection of essays by the Bishop of Peterborough.

The practice in the slaveholding section of America was to declare a week's holiday at Christmas. Jefferson's account book for December shows no special dispensation of gifts or cash to his blacks, unless the four French louis he gave Martha—who had come up from Varina with her husband—were for this purpose. But apparently the whole Monticello family, white and black, celebrated the coming emancipation of James Hemings. He would actually be freed February 6, when Jefferson would give him $30.00 and see him off to Philadelphia.

As the year drew to a close, it must have been apparent that his sabbatical was nearly over, although he continued the pretense that he was home to stay. To Edward Rutledge of South Carolina he wrote:

As the holidays approached, the kitchen was the scene of much activity. The Monticello kitchen is located beneath the south terrace walk. Courtesy of the Thomas Jefferson Memorial Foundation, Inc. (photograph by James Tkatch).

"You hope I have not abandoned entirely the service
of our country. After a five & twenty years continual
employment in it, I trust it will be thought I have ful-
filled my tour, like a punctual soldier, and may claim
my discharge."[46] If he was playing out a role, he was
staying in character until the bitter end. But 1796 was
upon him and it was an election year. His future was
not to be decided on the little mountain where he
lived, but in the halls of government in Philadelphia.

To the Republican leaders of Congress, Jefferson
was the only viable candidate for the presidency, and
they let him know it but were careful not to ask him
to run. He could have taken himself out of the race
but did not, and therein lies the uncertainty about his
ambiguous stand. Had it all been a game, or had Jay's
Treaty and the victories of Hamilton and the Federalists turned him around? He used a phrase that was
meaningful then, and even now, to men and women
who feel a responsibility to serve: he said he had
been "called out." As he was soon to write John
Langdon of New Hampshire, "I am happier at home
than I can be elsewhere. Since, however, I am called
out, an object of great anxiety to me is that those with
whom I am to act . . . will view me with the same
candor with which I shall certainly act."[47]

Jefferson may not have understood his own

behavior during his hiatus from government until a few years later. Maria, after her marriage, showed signs of withdrawing from society, and Jefferson wrote her about his own withdrawal:

> I am convinced our own happiness requires that we should continue to mix with the world, and to keep pace with it as it goes; and that every person who retires from free communication with it is severely punished afterwards by the state of mind into which they get, and which can only be prevented by feeding our sociable principles. I can speak from experience on this subject. From 1793. to 1797. I remained closely at home, saw none but those who came there, and at length became very sensible of the ill effect it had upon my own mind, and of it's direct and irresistible tendency to render me unfit for society, and uneasy when necessarily engaged in it. I felt enough of the effect of withdrawing from the world then, to see that it led to an antisocial and misanthropic state of mind, which severely punishes him who gives in to it: and it will be a lesson I never shall forget as to myself.[48]

Jefferson played no role in the approaching campaign, and it should be recalled that his own favorite
candidate to oppose the Federalists had been James
Madison. In the coming election he was to lose by
very few votes to Federalist John Adams, therefore
becoming vice-president. In 1801 he would become
the third president of the United States.

As if to prepare himself for reentry into that other
world, he did a natural thing. The day after Christmas
1795, he mailed $8.00 to publisher Bache for a year's
subscription to the *Aurora*. It was time to start catch-
ing up on the news.

Notes
and Sources

Notes

[1] Sarah N. Randolph, *The Domestic Life of Thomas Jefferson, Compiled from Family Letters and Reminiscences* (1871; Charlottesville: Published for the Thomas Jefferson Memorial Foundation by the University Press of Virginia, 1978), 231.

[2] Thomas Jefferson to Edmund Randolph, September 16, 1781, Julian P. Boyd, et al., eds., *The Papers of Thomas Jefferson* (23 vols.—; Princeton: Princeton University Press, 1950—), 6:118.

[3] Edmund Randolph to James Madison, May 10, 1782, quoted in ibid., 6:651n.

4 Thomas Jefferson to George Washington, December 15, 1789, ibid., 16:34, 35.

5 Thomas Mann Randolph to Thomas Jefferson, May 25, 1790, ibid., 16:441.

6 Thomas Jefferson to James Madison, June 9, 1793, Paul Leicester Ford, ed., *The Writings of Thomas Jefferson* (10 vols.; New York: G. P. Putnam's Sons, 1892-99), 6:291.

7 Thomas Jefferson to Martha Jefferson Randolph, January 26, 1793, Edwin Morris Betts and James Adam Bear, Jr., eds., *The Family Letters of Thomas Jefferson* (Columbia: University of Missouri Press, 1966), 110.

8 Thomas Jefferson to Colonel David Humphreys, March 22, 1793, A. A. Lipscomb and Albert Ellery Bergh, eds., *The Writings of Thomas Jefferson,* definitive ed. (20 vols.; Washington, D.C.: Issued under the auspices of the Thomas Jefferson Memorial Association, 1907), 9:51.

9 Thomas Jefferson to George Washington, May 14, 1794, quoted in Edwin Morris Betts, ed., *Thomas Jefferson's Garden Book, 1766-1824, with Relevant Extracts from His Other Writings* (Philadelphia: American Philosophical Society, 1944), 186.

10 Thomas Jefferson to Martha Jefferson Randolph, January 22, 1795, Betts and Bear, eds., *Family Letters,* 133.

[11] Thomas Jefferson to Maria Jefferson, September 20, 1785, ibid., 30.

[12] Thomas Jefferson to Maria Jefferson, July 25, 1790, ibid., 62.

[13] George Washington to Arthur Young, June 18, 1792, quoted in Donald Jackson, ed., *The Diaries of George Washington* (6 vols.; Charlottesville: University Press of Virginia, 1976-79), 1:xxxiii.

[14] Thomas Jefferson to James Madison, December 28, 1794, Ford, ed., *Writings of Thomas Jefferson,* 6:517, 519.

[15] John Adams to Thomas Jefferson, February 5, 1795, Lester J. Cappon, ed., *The Adams–Jefferson Letters: The Complete Correspondence Between Thomas Jefferson and Abigail and John Adams* (2 vols.; Chapel Hill: Published for the Institute of Early American History and Culture at Williamsburg, Virginia, by the University of North Carolina Press, 1959), 1:256.

[16] Thomas Jefferson to John Adams, February 6, 1795, ibid., 1:257.

[17] Thomas Jefferson to Ellen Randolph Coolidge, March 19, 1826, quoted in Betts, ed., *Garden Book,* 618.

[18] Martha Jefferson Randolph to Thomas Jefferson, June 26, 1793, Betts and Bear, eds., *Family Letters,* 121.

[19] Dumas Malone, *Jefferson and the Ordeal of Liberty,* vol. 3 of *Jefferson and His Time* (Boston: Little, Brown and Co., 1962), 192.

[20] James Madison to Thomas Jefferson, March 23, 1795, Robert A. Rutland, et al., eds., *The Papers of James Madison* (15 vols.—; Chicago and Charlottesville: University of Chicago Press and University Press of Virginia, 1962—), 15:493.

[21] The quotation is from Thomas Jefferson to James Barbour, March 5, 1816, Betts, ed., *Garden Book,* 556.

[22] Thomas Jefferson to Ferdinand Grand, December 28, 1786, quoted in ibid., 119.

[23] Betts, ed., *Garden Book,* 6.

[24] Thomas Jefferson to John Threlkeld, March 26, 1807, quoted in ibid., 345.

[25] Thomas Jefferson to William Branch Giles, April 27, 1795, quoted in ibid., 235.

[26] Thomas Jefferson to James Madison, April 27, 1795, Ford, ed., *Writings of Thomas Jefferson,* 7:9-11.

[27] Thomas Jefferson to John Adams, May 27, 1795, Cappon, ed., *Adams–Jefferson Letters,* 1:258.

[28] Thomas Jefferson to Jean-Nicholas Démeunier, April 29, 1795, quoted in Malone, *Jefferson and the Ordeal of Liberty,* 218.

[29] Thomas Jefferson to John Adams, May 27, 1795, Cappon, ed., *Adams–Jefferson Letters,* 1:258.

[30] Thomas Jefferson to General Henry Knox, June 1, 1795, Massachusetts Historical Society, Boston.

[31] John Breckenridge to Thomas Jefferson, July 25, 1795, quoted in Betts, ed., *Garden Book,* 237.

[32] See Thomas Jefferson to Maria Jefferson Randolph, July 31, 1795, Betts and Bear, eds., *Family Letters,* 134–35; Malone, *Jefferson and the Ordeal of Liberty,* 235-36; William H. Gaines, Jr., *Thomas Mann Randolph: Jefferson's Son-in-Law* (Baton Rouge: Louisiana State University Press, 1966), 44.

[33] Thomas Jefferson to Henry Tazewell, September 13, 1795, Ford, ed., *Writings of Thomas Jefferson,* 7:30.

[34] Thomas Jefferson to Mann Page, August 30, 1795, ibid., 7:25.

[35] Thomas Jefferson, *Notes on the State of Virginia,* ibid., 3:268.

36 Thomas Jefferson to Mann Page, August 30, 1795, ibid., 7:24.

37 Thomas Jefferson to John Dortie, October 1, 1811, quoted in Betts, ed., *Garden Book*, 462.

38 Thomas Jefferson to Maria Cosway, October 12, 1786, Boyd, et al., eds., *Papers of Thomas Jefferson*, 10:444.

39 Dumas Malone, *Jefferson and the Rights of Man*, vol. 2 of *Jefferson and His Time* (Boston: Little, Brown and Co., 1951), 72.

40 Thomas Jefferson to Maria Cosway, September 8, 1795, Helen Duprey Bullock, *My Head and My Heart: A Little History of Thomas Jefferson and Maria Cosway* (New York: G. P. Putnam's Sons, 1945), 142-43.

41 Thomas Jefferson to James Madison, September 21, 1795, Ford, ed., *Writings of Thomas Jefferson*, 7:32, 33.

42 George Washington to Thomas Jefferson, October 4, 1795, John C. Fitzpatrick, ed., *The Writings of George Washington, from the Original Manuscript Sources, 1745-1799* (39 vols.; Washington, D.C.: Government Printing Office, 1931-44), 34:325.

43 The verse disseminated by Callender can be found in Dumas Malone, *Jefferson the President: First Term, 1801-1805*, vol. 4 of *Jefferson and His Time* (Boston: Little,

Brown and Co., 1970), 214; the quotation from *Domestic Manners* is on 213. Fawn Brodie reprints part of the Bryant poem in *Thomas Jefferson: An Intimate History* (New York: W. W. Norton and Co., 1974), 419.

[44] Edward Weeks, review of *Thomas Jefferson: An Intimate History,* by Fawn Brodie, *Atlantic* 233 (April 1974):118.

[45] Thomas Jefferson to Comte de Volney, quoted in Malone, *Jefferson and the Ordeal of Liberty,* 236.

[46] Thomas Jefferson to Edward Rutledge, November 30, 1795, Ford, ed., *Writings of Thomas Jefferson,* 7:39.

[47] Thomas Jefferson to John Langdon, January 22, 1797, ibid., 7:112.

[48] Thomas Jefferson to Maria Jefferson Eppes, March 3, 1802, Betts and Bear, eds., *Family Letters,* 219.

A Note on Sources

A   lthough Jefferson cut short the time he spent at his
writing desk during his temporary retirement from
public life, he still sent and received many letters from
which a view of the activities at Monticello can be pieced
together. The main collection of his letters is that at the
Library of Congress; other manuscript sources include the
Coolidge Collection at the Massachusetts Historical Society, Boston; the Jefferson Collection at the Henry E.
Huntington Library and Art Gallery, San Marino, Califor-
nia; and the Jefferson Papers in the National Archives and
Records Administration, Washington, D.C.

The year 1795 has not yet been covered in Julian P.
Boyd, et al., eds., *The Papers of Thomas Jefferson* (23 vols.;

Princeton: Princeton University Press, 1950—). Older collections include Paul Leicester Ford, ed., *The Writings of Thomas Jefferson* (10 vols.; New York: G. P. Putnam's Sons, 1892-99) and A. A. Lipscomb and Albert Ellery Bergh, eds., *The Writings of Thomas Jefferson* (20 vols.; Washington, D.C.: Thomas Jefferson Memorial Association, 1903-5, 1907).

Published collections of letters are often valuable for the annotations made by the editors, such as Edwin M. Betts and James Adam Bear, Jr., eds., *The Family Letters of Thomas Jefferson* (Columbia: University of Missouri Press, 1966). Another specialized collection is Lester J. Cappon, ed., *The Adams–Jefferson Letters: The Complete Correspondence Between Thomas Jefferson and Abigail and John Adams* (2 vols.; Chapel Hill: Published for the Institute of Early American History and Culture at Williamsburg, Virginia, by the University of North Carolina Press, 1959).

Miscellaneous documents such as Jefferson's account, garden, and farm books are invaluable. *Jefferson's Memorandum Books: Accounts, with Legal Records and Miscellany, 1767–1826,* edited by James Adam Bear, Jr., and Lucia C. Stanton, were published in two volumes in 1987 by the Princeton University Press. For the others, see Edwin M. Betts, ed., *Thomas Jefferson's Garden Book, 1766-1824, with Relevant Extracts from His Other Writings* (Philadelphia: American Philosophical Society, 1944) and *Thomas Jefferson's Farm Book, with Commentary and Relevant Extracts from Other Writings* (Philadelphia: American Philosophical Society, 1953). Both have recently been reissued; see Robert C. Baron, ed., *The Garden and Farm Books of Thomas Jefferson* (Golden, Colo.: Fulcrum, 1987).

A few fine biographies of Jefferson are available. See especially Dumas Malone, *Thomas Jefferson and His Time* (6 vols.; Boston: Little, Brown and Co., 1948-81) and Merrill D. Peterson, ed., *Thomas Jefferson: A Reference Biography* (New York: Charles Scribner's Sons, 1986), written by specially chosen experts in particular aspects of Jefferson's life.

On Monticello, see Frederick D. Nichols and James Adam Bear, Jr., *Monticello: A Guidebook* (Charlottesville: University Press of Virginia, 1967); James Adam Bear, Jr., ed., *Jefferson at Monticello* (Charlottesville: University Press of Virginia, 1967); and Jack McLaughlin, *Jefferson and Monticello: The Biography of a Builder* (New York: Henry Holt and Co., 1988).